BILL GATES

COMPUTER KING

JOSEPHA SHERMAN

A Gateway Biography
The Millbrook Press
Brookfield, Connecticut

Published by The Millbrook Press, Inc.
2 Old New Milford Road
Brookfield, CT 06804
www.millbrookpress.com

Library of Congress Cataloging-in-Publication Data
Sherman, Josepha.
Bill Gates : computer king / Josepha Sherman.
p. cm. — (A Gateway biography)
Includes bibliographical references and index.
Summary: A biography of the developer of Microsoft, Bill Gates, with details of his
life and a look at the beginnings of the personal computer industry.
ISBN 0-7613-1771-6 (lib. bdg.)
1. Gates, Bill, 1955– 2. Businessmen—United States—Biography—Juvenile litera-
ture. [1. Gates, Bill, 1955– 2. Businessmen.] I. Title. II. Series.
HC102.5.G38 S54 2000
338.7'610053'092—dc21
[B] 00-021054

Cover photograph courtesy of Corbis-Bettmann

Photographs courtesy of AP/Wide World Photos: pp. 6, 42; Seth Poppel Yearbook
Archives: pp. 8, 9, 12 (both); Corbis/Sygma: pp. 17 (© Brooks Kraft), 34 (© Joe McNally),
36 (© Rick Maiman); © Microsoft: pp. 18, 19, 23, 32; Apple Computer, Inc.: p. 22 (both);
Corbis/Bettmann: p. 25; Ann Summa/Time, Inc.: p. 30; Liaison Agency: p. 35 (© Dirck
Halstead); Reuters/Archive Photos: pp. 38 (© Anthony Bolante), 41 (© Jeff Christensen)

BILL GATES

When Bill Gates was born, on the night of October 28, 1955, there were no such things as personal computers. Computers in 1955 were big machines that sometimes took up a whole room and used large disks that looked something like the big reels on an old-fashioned tape recorder. What's more, computers were slow by today's standards, with less power than some of today's new computerized toys. The early computers were also so expensive and difficult to operate that only big companies and a few universities could afford them. But there were going to be some amazing changes in computers and the way they operated in only a few years. And Bill Gates was going to be one of the main reasons for those changes.

As Gates grew up in his home city of Seattle, Washington, he was surrounded by a family that was happy and well-to-do. His full name was William H. Gates III, but his parents and two sisters often just

BACK IN 1950 THIS COMPUTER WAS REFERRED TO AS AN "ELECTRIC BRAIN." THE ACCOMPANYING ARTICLE NOTED THAT IT WEIGHED 6,000 POUNDS (2,722 KG), HAD 25 MILES (42 KM) OF WIRES, AND 2,500 ELECTRICAL SWITCHES AND CONTACTS.

called him "Trey," because he was the third Bill Gates in a row. His father, Bill Gates II, was a lawyer and still is a philanthropist, who is someone who gives large sums of money to charity, and his mother served on the boards of banks and charities. Gates says, "I was fortunate enough to be raised in a family that encouraged kids to ask questions."

Gates did ask questions. He was one of the brightest boys in elementary school—so bright that he could get an A in almost any subject without having to study. At age eight, he even decided to read the entire *World Book Encyclopedia*, and made it as far as the letter P before stopping.

Bright boy though he was, Bill Gates showed right from the start that he wasn't going to be like anyone else. He wasn't a bad boy. But he would get into so many arguments with everyone, including his mother, that his parents grew worried. Was there something wrong with his mind?

They sent their son to a child psychiatrist. But the psychiatrist quickly realized that there was nothing wrong with Gates. He was simply a strong-willed, very intelligent boy who loved to compete. This didn't mean that he was headed toward a sports career. Gates wasn't tall or muscular. Where he excelled was in tests of the mind.

So Gates's parents took him out of public school as soon as he'd finished sixth grade, and sent him to a private school called the Lakeside School, which had high academic standards.

This turned out to be the best move they could ever have made for their son, but not in any way they could have planned. In the spring of 1968, Lakeside became one of the first schools to provide computer time for the students. Since computers in 1968 were still large and expensive, the school couldn't afford to own one. Instead, Lakeside bought time on a computer owned by General Electric.

PAUL ALLEN MUST HAVE BEEN A PUZZLE TO HIS TEACHERS, AND NOT JUST BECAUSE HE WAS SO BRIGHT. HERE HE'S IN HIS "ELECTRIC CHAIR" FOR A CANDID YEARBOOK SHOT WHEN BOTH HE AND BILL GATES WERE IN EIGHTH GRADE.

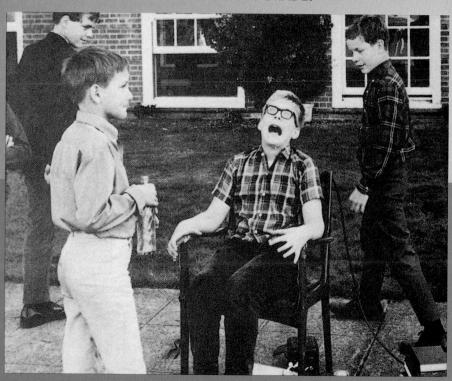

The school could only afford to rent the computer for a few hours a week. But Bill Gates and his friends, fellow students Paul Allen and Kent Evans, were delighted. They spent as much time as they could in the computer room, night and day, learning everything they could about computers. Sometimes they used up the school's computer time all by themselves. Sometimes they forgot all about homework, or attending classes!

0101010101010101010101010101

A computer is just a machine. It is sometimes called "hardware," since it's a solid object. Like any other machine, it can't do anything without instructions. A computer's instructions are called programs, or "software," since instructions aren't solid objects.

Nowadays, anyone who wants to add new instructions to a computer can just go to a computer store and buy a software package. There are programs to solve math problems, or teach a new language, or just play games. Back in 1968, there were no stores selling software for computers. Computer users had to write their own programs. Gates's very first computer program, which he wrote at age thirteen, was a simple game of tic-tac-toe. It probably would have been faster to play with pen and paper—but it worked!

Six months after the Lakeside School first made computer time available to the students, a company called Computer Center Corporation offered computer time at a lower cost—and on a better machine.

Bill Gates and his friends were overjoyed. Their explorations and experiments with this new computer caused the computer to crash, or temporarily stop working, several times. The boys also managed to change some files on the computer to make it look as though they weren't spending so much time there. But someone noticed the changed files. Gates and his friends were banned from the computer for several miserable weeks.

In 1968, while they were still students, Bill Gates, Paul Allen, and Kent Evans formed their own company. They named it the Lakeside Programmers Group. And they found a customer right away. Computer Center Corporation or, as Gates called it, "C-Cubed," meaning C three times, knew that its computers were crashing too often. So it hired the Lakeside Programmers Group to fix the problem. In exchange, the boys were given unlimited computer time.

It was wonderful. Now they could not only fix bugs, which are what errors in computer programs are called, but also could learn more about computing. And no one would tell them they were wasting time!

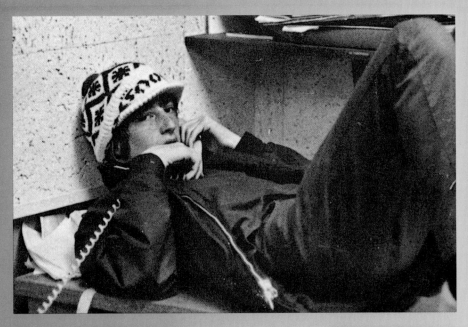

In 1971, Bill Gates (above) and Paul Allen completed their senior year at Lakeside.

Unfortunately, C-Cubed went out of business in 1970. The Lakeside Programmers Group went looking for another customer. And they found their first paying job. A company called Information Sciences Inc. hired them to create a payroll program for its computer. Now the Lakeside Programmers Group was a real business!

Then something terrible happened. Kent Evans died in a mountain climbing accident. Gates was so full of grief that, as he says, "for two weeks, I couldn't do anything at all."

Then Gates and Allen went to work again. Maybe Evans's death made them work even harder. Allen, who is a year older than Gates, went to college in Pullman, Washington, but the two friends stayed close. They formed a new company, Traf-O-Data, and began working summers on computer programming jobs. They did very well. In fact, they earned $20,000 while still in school!

One summer job was with TRW, a company working for the United States military. As Gates remembered, the job was "to find ways to crash its system—fun for eager young programmers." And it was during this job that Gates and Allen came up with the idea of forming their own software company. But that would have to wait until after Gates finished college.

In 1973, Bill Gates left Seattle to attend Harvard University in Cambridge, Massachusetts. What was he going to study? Harvard didn't offer any degrees in computer science in 1973. Gates majored in prelaw, the beginning courses for someone who wants to become a lawyer.

But just as he did in elementary school and high school, Gates quickly lost interest in what he was supposed to be studying. Instead, he spent as much time as he could in Harvard's computer center. Sometimes he was there until late into the night—and sometimes he'd fall asleep in class the next day!

Gates stayed in close touch with his friend, Paul Allen. Allen found a computer job near Harvard during Gates's first year in college, at a company called Honeywell. That summer, Gates got a job there, too. He and Allen continued to talk over the idea of having their own software company. But Gates knew that if they did start up a company, he wouldn't have the time to stay in college. Should he stay and get his degree? After all, computers just didn't have enough power to run the software he and Allen wanted to design.

Then Paul Allen saw an article in the January 1975 issue of a magazine called *Popular Electronics*. "This is it!" he cried to Gates. "It's about to begin." The cover headline read, "Project Breakthrough! World's First Microcomputer Kit to Rival Commercial Models."

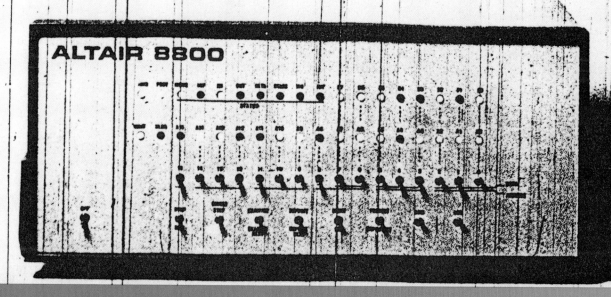

THE AD IN *POPULAR ELECTRONICS* FOR THE ALTAIR 8800, WHICH
CAUGHT THE EYE OF PAUL ALLEN.

The article was about a new computer named the Altair. It wasn't very fast or very powerful. But it was the first personal computer—the first computer small enough to be used by just one person, rather than by a company.

Now other companies were sure to start building personal computers. The computer world was about to change forever. Gates and Allen knew that if they didn't start their software company now, they were going to be left behind.

Gates thought quickly. He telephoned MITS, the company that had invented the Altair. He told them that he knew they didn't have any software programs for the Altair. He claimed he had a new form of BASIC that would run their computer. BASIC stands for Beginner's All-Purpose Symbolic Instruction Code. It's a language of numbers, not words, a code used in programming computers.

When Bill Gates made his phone call, neither he nor Allen had created one line of new BASIC code. They didn't even own an Altair! But Gates did such a good job of selling that MITS was eager to see the BASIC program. Now Gates and Allen had a lot of fast work to do! Gates started creating a usable BASIC program, while Allen did the best he could to make Harvard's computers act like Altairs so that Gates and he could test their hastily written program.

THE COMPUTER MUSEUM, IN BOSTON, MASSACHUSETTS,
ARRANGED THIS SPACE TO LOOK LIKE A COMPUTER HACKER'S
GARAGE WOULD HAVE LOOKED IN 1970.

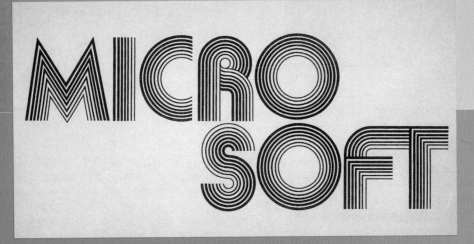

It worked. In February 1975, MITS bought the BASIC program. Gates and Allen had created the first computer program for a personal computer. By June 1975, Gates dropped out of Harvard, and he and Allen finally formed their software company.

What could they call it? They wanted a name that would make people think at the same time of personal computers and software. Toward the end of 1975, they came up with the name "Micro-soft," then condensed it to Microsoft. The "Micro" part stood for "microcomputers," personal computers like the Altair. The "soft" part stood for "software."

Where were they going to put their brand-new company? In 1976, Gates and Allen decided on Albuquerque, New Mexico. MITS had its headquarters in Albuquerque. It was also cheaper to live in New Mexico. And maybe a small part of the decision had to do with all that empty desert space! Whenever he had a little free time, Gates loved to race his car out over the open desert.

Gates and Allen had started up Microsoft at just the right time. Many new computer companies were being

A PHOTOGRAPH OF THE ALBUQUERQUE GROUP. BILL GATES IN ON THE LEFT IN THE FRONT ROW, AND PAUL ALLEN IS ON THE RIGHT.

created to rival MITS, and they all needed software. Gates spent long days and nights designing this software, sometimes working eighteen hours straight. There were nights when he didn't even bother going home, but slept curled up under his desk.

He was having fun. And Microsoft was making money. But Microsoft soon had too much work for even someone like Bill Gates. He and Allen hired their first employees. These were all eager young people, excited about working on computer programs. They didn't mind having to work the long hours. They didn't even mind having to bring sleeping bags to the office when they knew that a project would take almost all night.

In 1977, Gates and Allen signed an agreement making Microsoft a legal partnership, a business owned by two people. Was this deal made because they were always quarreling? Any two good friends do fight from time to time. And any fights between Gates and Allen never got in the way of friendship—or business.

That year, Gates and Allen had trouble with MITS over the BASIC program that Gates had written. MITS had agreed to license the program, which meant renting it out, to other companies. That meant that both MITS and Microsoft would make money every time the program was used. But Gates and Allen didn't think MITS was doing a good job of getting the program to other companies. A judge ruled in Microsoft's favor. Now Gates was free to market his BASIC program himself. Other companies wanted it, and money started coming into Microsoft on a regular basis.

In the next few years, many new computer companies were started. Many failed just as quickly. But some became very successful, like Radio Shack and Commodore. The most successful new company was called Apple Computer. This company was cofounded by two young men named Steve Jobs and Steve Wozniak. Like Bill Gates, both Jobs and Wozniak had dropped out of college to found the company. Steve Wozniak, who went to work for Hewlett Packard, did all the computer work, while Jobs focused on the business of marketing Apple. Also like Bill Gates, they quickly became wealthy. In 1977, Jobs and Wozniak put out a very successful new computer, the Apple II. MITS and their Altair computer were soon out of date.

Gates knew that the computer rush wasn't happening only in the United States. So in 1978 he made Microsoft's first international deal, opening a Microsoft partner office in Tokyo, Japan.

By December 1978, Microsoft had so much business that it had outgrown the space it could get in

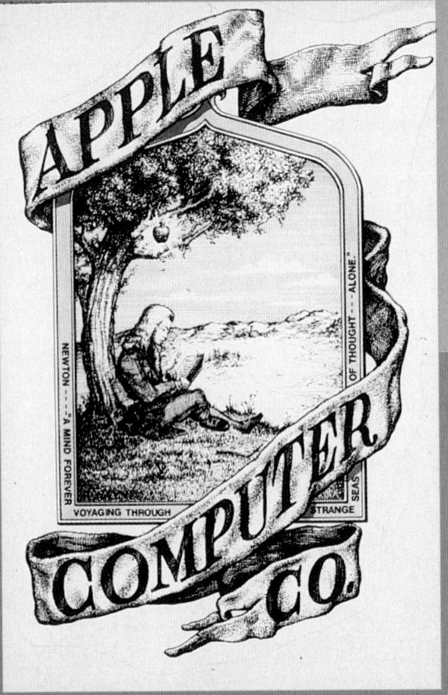

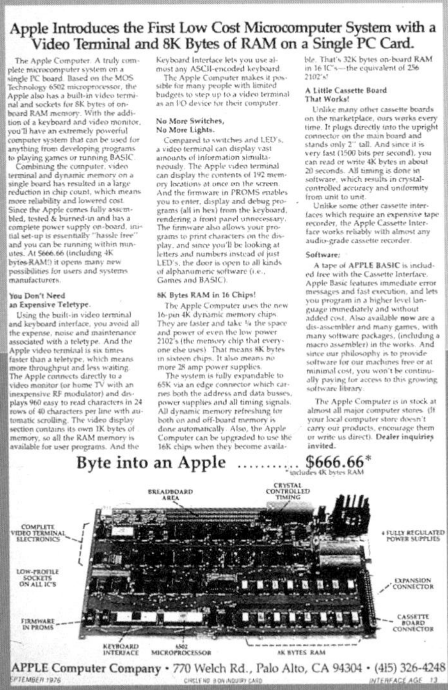

Apple Introduces the First Low Cost Microcomputer System with a Video Terminal and 8K Bytes of RAM on a Single PC Card.

The Apple Computer. A truly complete microcomputer system on a single PC board. Based on the MOS Technology 6502 microprocessor, the Apple also has a built-in video terminal and sockets for 8K bytes of on-board RAM memory. With the addition of a keyboard and video monitor, you'll have an extremely powerful computer system that can be used for anything from developing programs to playing games or running BASIC.

Combining the computer, video terminal and dynamic memory on a single board has resulted in a large reduction in chip count, which means more reliability and lowered cost. Since the Apple comes fully assembled, tested & burned-in and has a complete power supply on-board, initial set-up is essentially "hassle free" and you can be running within minutes. At $666.66 (including 4K bytes RAM!) it opens many new possibilities for users and systems manufacturers.

You Don't Need an Expensive Teletype.

Using the built-in video terminal and keyboard interface, you avoid all the expense, noise and maintenance associated with a teletype. And the Apple video terminal is six times faster than a teletype, which means more throughput and less waiting. The Apple connects directly to a video monitor (or home TV with an inexpensive RF modulator) and displays 960 easy to read characters in 24 rows of 40 characters per line with automatic scrolling. The video display section contains its own 1K bytes of memory, so all the RAM memory is available for user programs. And the Keyboard Interface lets you use almost any ASCII-encoded keyboard.

The Apple Computer makes it possible for many people with limited budgets to step up to a video terminal as an I/O device for their computer.

No More Switches, No More Lights.

Compared to switches and LED's, a video terminal can display vast amounts of information simultaneously. The Apple video terminal can display the contents of 192 memory locations at once on the screen. And the firmware in PROMS enables you to enter, display and debug programs (all in hex) from the keyboard, rendering a front panel unnecessary. The firmware also allows your programs to print characters on the display, and since you'll be looking at letters and numbers instead of just LED's, the door is open to all kinds of alphanumeric software (i.e., Games and BASIC).

8K Bytes RAM in 16 Chips!

The Apple Computer uses the new 16-pin 4K dynamic memory chips. They are faster and take ¼ the space and power of even the low power 2102's (the memory chip that everyone else uses). That means 8K bytes in sixteen chips. It also means no more 28 amp power supplies.

The system is fully expandable to 65K via an edge connector which carries both the address and data busses, power supplies and all timing signals. All dynamic memory refreshing for both on and off-board memory is done automatically. Also, the Apple Computer can be upgraded to use the 16K chips when they become available. That's 32K bytes on-board RAM in 16 IC's—the equivalent of 256 2102's!

A Little Cassette Board That Works!

Unlike many other cassette boards on the marketplace, ours works every time. It plugs directly into the upright connector on the main board and stands only 2" tall. And since it is very fast (1500 bits per second), you can read or write 4K bytes in about 20 seconds. All timing is done in software, which results in crystal-controlled accuracy and uniformity from unit to unit.

Unlike some other cassette interfaces which require an expensive tape recorder, the Apple Cassette Interface works reliably with almost any audio-grade cassette recorder.

Software:

A tape of **APPLE BASIC** is included free with the Cassette Interface. Apple Basic features immediate error messages and fast execution, and lets you program in a higher level language immediately and without added cost. Also available **now** are a dis-assembler and many games, with many software packages, (including a macro assembler) in the works. And since our philosophy is to provide software for our machines free or at minimal cost, you won't be continually paying for access to this growing software library.

The Apple Computer is in stock at almost all major computer stores. (If your local computer store doesn't carry our products, encourage them or write us direct). **Dealer inquiries invited.**

Byte into an Apple $666.66*

*includes 4K bytes RAM

BREADBOARD AREA
CRYSTAL CONTROLLED TIMING
COMPLETE VIDEO TERMINAL ELECTRONICS
4 FULLY REGULATED POWER SUPPLIES
LOW-PROFILE SOCKETS ON ALL IC'S
EXPANSION CONNECTOR
FIRMWARE IN PROMS
CASSETTE BOARD CONNECTOR
KEYBOARD INTERFACE
6502 MICROPROCESSOR
8K BYTES RAM

APPLE Computer Company • 770 Welch Rd., Palo Alto, CA 94304 • (415) 326-4248

EPTEMBER 1976 CIRCLE NO. 9 ON INQUIRY CARD INTERFACE AGE 13

THE FIRST LOGO FOR APPLE COMPUTERS AND THEIR FIRST ADVERTISEMENT.

Albuquerque. Gates moved Microsoft to Bellevue, Washington, which is a suburb of his home city, Seattle. Now the company, which had grown to more than thirty employees, had room to expand.

As personal computers became more complicated and more powerful during 1979, Microsoft created a more powerful version of BASIC for them. Gates also made a European deal, creating a Microsoft partnership in Belgium. But Gates knew Microsoft had to keep finding new markets and creating new products. Computer languages weren't going to be all that new-comers to personal computers were going to want. What about those who wanted to use computers instead of typewriters? What about those who wanted to run financial programs or do bookkeeping work on computers? People were already creating simple games for computers, with words but no pictures, but Gates wasn't really happy with this side of the industry yet.

PAUL ALLEN AND BILL GATES IN 1981, SURROUNDED BY EARLY-MODEL PERSONAL COMPUTERS.

The IBM Corporation was already a large, wealthy company. In 1980, IBM entered the personal computer field. They wanted a new operating system for their new computers, and Gates was ready. He told the IBM executives that he had exactly what they wanted.

Did he? Yes and no! Gates knew that a small company called Seattle Computer Products had invented a good new computer operating system they called Q-DOS. The name DOS stands for (Computer) Disk Operating System. Seattle Computer Products didn't know that IBM was looking for a system like theirs. So Gates bought this system for only $50,000. That wasn't as expensive as it sounds. The system, which Gates renamed MS-DOS, for Microsoft Disk Operating System, quickly earned him his first million dollars.

Gates was clever. He didn't let IBM buy MS-DOS. They could only license it. Gates knew that other computer companies were designing similar machines. Because he hadn't sold MS-DOS, he was free to license it to these other companies as well.

IBM was run by people who wanted everyone to play by their rules. They wanted a system called OS/2 to be the one to run their computers. Bill Gates didn't think much of this system, and he didn't work well with the IBM people. His MS-DOS really was a good program, and it soon became the most popular program in computing—with one exception.

FROM THE LEFT, STEVE JOBS, COFOUNDER OF APPLE, JOHN SCULLEY, PRESIDENT, AND STEVE WOZNIAK, COFOUNDER. THIS 1984 PHOTOGRAPH WAS TAKEN AT A TRADE SHOW AT WHICH APPLE INTRODUCED THEIR BRIEFCASE-SIZE APPLE II COMPUTER.

That exception came with the computers made by Steve Jobs's company, Apple Computers. Gates decided that Apple should use Microsoft software, too. After all, Microsoft had already designed one computer program for the Apple in 1980.

Gates and Jobs met in 1981. By this point, both young men were quite wealthy, each worth several million dollars. But they were very different. Gates enjoyed being a computer "nerd," someone who worked directly on computer programs. Jobs liked giving orders. He wanted Microsoft to design programs for his new Macintosh computer, nicknamed the Mac. Gates pretended to be thinking about it. To win Gates over, Jobs had a Macintosh computer delivered to Microsoft's offices before Macs were sold to the public. In 1982, Gates and Jobs agreed that Microsoft would work on programs for the Mac.

What made the Macintosh special? Its operating system was very different. With the MS-DOS program, a computer user had to type in every command. This meant remembering long lines of letters and symbols. To open a program on a Macintosh, the computer user used a gooey, after GUI—graphic user interface. The main part of the gooey was the screen, which allowed the user to point and click to open a program or a file. The pointing and clicking was done with a mouse. It's called that because it's usually gray, with a thin, tail-like cord, and does look a little like a real mouse! Apple Computer didn't invent the mouse. Both the mouse and gooey were created by the Xerox Corporation.

With a mouse, anyone with a Macintosh could click on any "icon," a little picture on the computer screen, to open a program. This was much faster than MS-DOS. There were no long strings of letters to remember.

But suddenly there was a major change in Microsoft's ownership and in Bill Gates's life. Paul Allen was diagnosed with cancer. He made a full recovery. But he no longer wanted the stress of the computer world. So Allen left Microsoft in 1983. Since then, he has owned several businesses, including the Portland Trail Blazers basketball team. Allen also donates a great deal to charity. And Bill Gates and he remain good friends.

Did Gates miss having his friend working with him? He said, "It was great that Paul got better, and we wanted him to come back more than anything." But he also added that anyone at Microsoft would have to be prepared to work hard. In fact, some people think that without Allen working with Gates at Microsoft, Gates became more than hardworking. They say he became too competitive.

Or was he merely being a very clever businessman? In November 1983, Microsoft announced a new product: Microsoft Windows. This was a new form of operating system, using icons on the screen rather than the MS-DOS method of typing in commands. The Macintosh also used icons. Microsoft Windows used the Microsoft mouse. The Macintosh also used a mouse.

The lawyers at Apple Computer threatened to sue. They accused Microsoft of stealing their ideas! Gates countered that Apple had already borrowed the idea of the mouse, and maybe even the idea of icons as well, from Xerox. Besides, Apple had legally agreed that Microsoft would write software for the Mac.

A deal was struck. Gates licensed the right to keep his Windows program looking like that of the Mac. And Microsoft did develop software for the Mac. Gates knew exactly what he was doing. Now his Windows program would be able to advance. And at the same time, Microsoft was still designing software for its rival!

In 1985, Microsoft celebrated its tenth anniversary. In ten years, it had grown to over 1,000 employees. That year, Microsoft products earned more than $140 million.

But Microsoft Windows wasn't doing very well. Most software programs were still being written for MS-DOS or the Macintosh. There were too few software programs that would work with Windows.

Gates wasn't discouraged. This was, after all, a new design. There would soon be new and better versions of Windows. Meanwhile, Microsoft's programmers were busy creating the first version of Microsoft Works for the Macintosh. This was a combination of software programs, including one for word processing, or writing on the computer, and several for businesses. Such software packages are known as suites. Since it's handy to have so many programs in one package, suites have become very popular.

Gates's company was rapidly outgrowing the Bellevue offices. In 1986, Microsoft moved to Redmond, Washington, about 15 miles (24 kilometers) from Seattle. Gates named his new headquarters the Microsoft Corporate Campus, made up of Buildings 1 through 4. Now there would finally be plenty of room!

This was also the year in which Gates opened a branch of Microsoft in Mexico. Now he had branches of Microsoft in Latin America, Europe, and Asia.

And this was the year in which Bill Gates became a billionaire. He was only thirty-one!

Now that he had so much money, Gates decided to be like his father and give money to charity. Together with Paul Allen, Gates gave over $2 million to the

BILL GATES'S FATHER, BILL GATES JR., IS VERY MUCH INVOLVED IN HIS SON'S PHILANTHROPIC CONTRIBUTIONS.

Lakeside School for a new science and mathematics building. It's called Allen-Gates Hall.

In 1987, Gates met a young woman named Melinda French, a general manager for Microsoft. And they started dating.

The next business step for Gates was to get Microsoft Windows upgraded. The new version was called Windows 2.0, and it was better than the first one. But it still wasn't very successful. Had Gates made a big mistake?

Microsoft continued to make money, though. By 1987, it was the number one seller of computer software. The Corporate Campus soon wasn't big enough! It was expanded from four to eight buildings, then expanded again. Today, there are forty-nine buildings set in a 29-acre (12-hectare) park that even has a basketball court and a baseball field for Microsoft workers!

IBM was still a problem for Gates. IBM insisted that OS/2, not Microsoft Windows, would be its main computer operating system. The arguments were too much for Gates! In 1989 he broke off all Microsoft deals with IBM. The OS/2 system still exists. But IBM has never made it a true success.

Meanwhile, Gates issued a new version of Microsoft Windows, 3.0. It still wasn't that popular. But Bill Gates had always been a fighter, and he wasn't going to back down now. He launched an enormous advertising campaign for Windows, spending over $10 million in six months. It was the largest advertising campaign in Microsoft's history. And people began to really notice Microsoft Windows.

THE MICROSOFT CAMPUS TODAY, IN SEATTLE, WASHINGTON

So did the Federal Trade Commission. This branch of the United States government looks out for any breaking of business laws. One of those is called the Anti-Trust Law, and it means that no one company can unfairly dominate its rivals. This was the first time that Microsoft and Bill Gates were questioned by the Federal Trade Commission—but it wasn't going to be the last. This time, the Federal Trade Commission ruled that Microsoft and Gates weren't doing anything wrong.

In 1992 the final papers were signed marking the break between Microsoft and IBM. Everyone at Microsoft must have been nervous. Gates seemed to be gambling the whole company on the newest version of Windows, Microsoft Windows 3.1.

It wasn't really a gamble. People paid attention to the advertising, and they wanted Windows 3.1. It was installed on 70 million computers in 1992. Software companies began writing most of their programs to run with Windows.

Microsoft was still writing its own software, too. Microsoft Encarta, which first appeared in 1993, was the first encyclopedia designed for the computer. Updated every year, it has become a bestseller.

Bill Gates had another victory in 1993. The last lawsuit filed by Apple Computer against Microsoft was settled, and Microsoft won. *Fortune Magazine*, a leading business publication, voted Microsoft "the 1993 Most Innovative Company Operating in the U.S."

By 1994, Microsoft Windows 3.1 was the operating system on 90 percent of the computers people

BILL GATES, AT AGE THIRTY-THREE IN 1989, WAS THE WORLD'S YOUNGEST BILLIONAIRE.

ONE CHANGE BROUGHT TO THE AMERICAN WORKPLACE BY PEOPLE WHO WORKED ON DEVELOPING NEW COMPUTERS AND SOFTWARE WAS THE FREEDOM TO RELAX AND BE YOURSELF IN THE OFFICE.

bought. But Gates knew that Windows still wasn't as good as it could be. He scheduled a new version, Windows 95, for 1994, but the program was too big and complicated to be ready that year.

Bill Gates's personal life was pretty complicated in 1994, too. His mother died from cancer. But there was joy as well. Gates and Melinda French, who had been dating for six years, were married on January 1, 1994.

MELINDA GATES

Gates started planning their dream house on Lake Washington in Seattle. The house is still being built. When it's finally finished, it will be almost completely computerized, and include a movie theater, an indoor swimming pool, and every type of technology that Bill Gates can imagine.

Microsoft Windows 95 appeared in 1995. And it was a best-seller. Windows 95 sold more than a million copies in the first four days it was on sale! By October 1995 there were about 7 million copies of the program around the world.

In November 1995, Bill Gates's first book, *The Road Ahead*, was published. It was Gates's view on how the world was going to change through the computer and the Internet. All profit from this book went to charity.

Bill Gates's personal life changed in 1996. He and his wife became the parents of a baby girl they named Jennifer. Gates loved being a daddy!

But he was still the active head of Microsoft. He looked for new ways for Microsoft to expand, this time into the Internet. Bill Gates sees the Internet both as a force for learning and as a source of income. He's said, "The information age is opening up new possibilities for all of us, for our children and for the entire nation."

So Microsoft developed its own Internet browser, Microsoft Explorer. An Internet browser is a software program that lets someone get onto the Internet. A rival company, Netscape, has its own Internet browser, called Netscape Navigator. A lawsuit was filed in 1996 by the owners of Netscape. They claimed that Microsoft included Microsoft Explorer with every copy of Windows. They also claimed that Gates wanted to force Netscape out of business. Was this true? The case is still being examined.

Meanwhile, Microsoft and NBC News teamed up to create MSNBC, a twenty-four-hour news network on the Internet. Microsoft also bought WebTV Networks, which will let people get onto the Internet through their televisions. Microsoft's own Web site was expanded as well, and now offers information on the company, and on Bill Gates and his charities.

One of those charities, the Gates Library Initiative, was founded in 1997. This program makes grants to public libraries in the United States and Canada, allowing them to buy computers and access to the

BILL AND MELINDA'S HOME ON LAKE WASHINGTON.

Internet. The grants include free assistance from the Gates Center for Technology Access.

Meanwhile, Steve Jobs, who started up Apple Computers, wasn't doing as well as Gates. His company made a series of bad choices, such as the 1993 Newton, which was a handheld computer that just didn't work very well. Things got so bad that Jobs was fired from his own company! Jobs and Apple Computer saw Microsoft and Bill Gates as an enemy. But when Jobs was invited back to Apple in 1997, the only way for Apple to exist was to allow Gates to buy part of the company. Apple Computer is now successful once more.

By 1998, Bill Gates had become a billionaire so many times over that he was the wealthiest man in the world! He was worth over $40 billion, and by now may be worth over $90 billion. That's almost too much money to imagine! Gates decided that he would do his best to give away 95 percent of it. He had already donated $135 million to medicine and education, and was ranked as the number three philanthropist in the United States.

Melinda Gates is as interested in charity as her husband. She helps manage the many Gates charitable organizations. In fact, they are now known as the Bill and Melinda Gates Foundations. Gates's father is also active in running the William H. Gates Foundation. In

1999, Gates donated an amazing $6 billion dollars to these foundations.

Part of the job of the Bill and Melinda Gates foundations is to give more people access to education. Gates has personally donated $15 million to Harvard University for a new computer center, $6 million to Stanford University, and $34 million to the University of Washington in Seattle. He believes that a good education is the best way to end poverty.

Another main aim of the foundations is making the world a healthier place. Gates has started a fund to see that children all around the world, particularly in the poorest countries, are immunized against disease. And he donates to the fight against cancer.

Meanwhile, Microsoft continues to make news. In 1998, Microsoft Windows 98 appeared. Still another version, Microsoft Windows 2000, was originally scheduled to be issued in 1999. But like Windows 95 and 98, it was too complicated to be finished on time. Also in 1998 the United States Justice Department began to investigate Microsoft once again. The Justice Department claims that Microsoft isn't leaving room for other companies. Is this claim true? Or is Microsoft simply better at what it does? The case is still going on, and no one knows when or how it will end.

In 1999, Bill Gates published his second book, *Business @ the Speed of Thought.* It's about the ways

MELINDA AND BILL GATES LISTEN TO FIFTEEN-YEAR-OLD JOSH STACK EXPLAIN HIS TOWN LIBRARY'S WEB SITE. THE GATESES HAVE BEEN GENEROUS IN DONATING FUNDS FOR EDUCATION AND LIBRARIES ACROSS THE COUNTRY.

business can make use of the Internet and the new electronics. The profits of this book, too, are being donated to charity.

Another new arrival appeared in 1999. Gates and his wife had a second child, a boy they named Rory John.

Has Bill Gates changed now that he is so amazingly wealthy? Not really! He says, "I choose each day to do

BILL GATES IN FRONT OF THE SENATE JUDICIARY COMMITTEE IN 1998, ANSWERING CHARGES THAT MICROSOFT WAS UNFAIRLY TRYING TO CORNER THE MARKET ON INTERNET ACCESS.

exactly what I'm doing." Gates still likes to work with computers and computer programming. And he thinks nothing of dressing like anyone else, or going for a walk as though he were just another ordinary person.

But Bill Gates will never be ordinary. No one knows what will come of the Justice Department case against Microsoft. No one knows what new plans Gates has in store, either. The only thing that seems certain is that Bill Gates will be remembered in the next century as one of the major shapers of this one.

IMPORTANT DATES

1955	Bill Gates is born on October 28, 1955, in Seattle, Washington.
1968	Gates writes his first computer program, and forms the Lakeside Programmers Group.
1973	Gates attends Harvard University in Cambridge, Massachusetts.
1974	The Altair, the first personal computer, is invented and sold as a kit.
	Bill Gates and Paul Allen sell MITS their BASIC program for the Altair.
1975	Gates drops out of Harvard University.
	Gates and Paul Allen found Microsoft.
1976	Microsoft moves to Albuquerque, New Mexico.
1977	Steve Jobs and Apple Computer create the Apple II.
1977–1978	Microsoft breaks with MITS and begins selling to other companies.
1979	Microsoft moves to new offices in Bellevue, Washington.

1980	Gates buys Q-DOS, renames it MS-DOS, and licenses it to IBM.
1982	Bill Gates and Steve Jobs agree that Microsoft will write software for Jobs's Macintosh Computer.
1983	Paul Allen leaves Microsoft. The first version of Microsoft Windows appears.
1983–84	Gates settles with Steve Jobs's lawyers. Windows stays on the market.
1985	Microsoft celebrates its tenth anniversary.
1986	Microsoft moves to larger offices in Redmond, Washington. Gates becomes a billionaire at age thirty-one. Gates makes his first big charitable contribution.
1987	Bill Gates and Melinda French meet. Microsoft becomes the number one software company.
1989	Microsoft breaks with IBM. The Federal Trade Commission investigates Microsoft.
1993	Microsoft Windows 3.1 is issued.
1994	Bill Gates and Melinda French are married. Gates' mother dies of cancer. Gates begins building a dream house for his family.
1995	Microsoft Windows 95 appears and is a best-seller. Gates's first book, *The Road Ahead*, is published. Gates is now the richest man in the world.
1996	Gates's first child, Jennifer, is born.

1997	Gates starts setting up his charitable organizations, such as the Gates Foundation.
	Microsoft buys part of Apple Computer.
1999	Gates's second child, Rory John, is born.
	Gates's second book, *Business @ the Speed of Thought*, is published.
2000	Microsoft Windows 2000 becomes available
Ongoing	The Department of Justice investigates Microsoft.

FURTHER READING

ABOUT BILL GATES

Gatlin, Jonathan. *Bill Gates: The Path to the Future*. New York: Avon Books, 1999.

McIntosh, I.B. *Microman: What Life Might Be Like If You Were Bill Gates*. Chicago: Arsenal Pulp Press Login Pub., 1998.

Simon, Charnan. *Bill Gates: Helping People Use Computers*. Minneapolis: Children's Press, 1997.

BOOKS BY BILL GATES

Business @ the Speed of Thought. New York: Warner Books, 1999.

The Road Ahead. New York: Wheeler Publications, 1996.

WEB SITES ABOUT MICROSOFT AND BILL GATES

www.microsoft.com This is the main Microsoft webpage.

www.microsoft.com/kids/ This is Microsoft's site for kids. Plenty of activities, and a link to Scholastic, Inc., the book publisher.

www.microsoft.com/billgates/ This is Bill Gates's own site. You can read his own views and ideas here.

SILLY BOOK ABOUT BILL GATES AND MICROSOFT

Alpine, Chris. *Bill Gates 99: Paper Doll Book*. New York: St. Martin's Press, 1998.

INDEX